Words on the Winds

In this collection you will find ballads old and new, each one chosen for its special power to excite your interest, capture your imagination, and send its echoes through your mind long after you have turned the page.

Cover illustration by Desmond Clover

Words on the Winds

A book of ballads
compiled by
Dennis Saunders

Evans Brothers Limited London

Published by Evans Brothers Limited
Montague House, Russell Square,
London W.C.1.

To Pam, my wife

Set in 11 on 13 pt Imprint and
printed in Great Britain by
Cox & Wyman Ltd,
London, Reading and Fakenham

CSD ISBN 0 237 44756 8   PRA 3565
PB   ISBN 0 237 44757 6

Contents

The Wife of Usher's Well

There lived a wife at Usher's Well,
    And a wealthy wife was she;
She had three stout and stalwart sons,
    And sent them o'er the sea.

They had not been a week from her,
    A week but barely one,
When word came to that carline wife
    That her three sons were gone.

They had not been a week from her,
    A week but barely three,
When word came to that carline wife
    That her sons she'd never see.

'I wish the wind may never cease,
    Nor troubles in the flood,
Till my three sons come home to me
    In earthly flesh and blood!'

It fell about the Martinmas,
    When the nights are long and murk,
That the carline wife's three sons came home,
    And their hats were of the birk.

carline: old
birk: birch

It neither grew in marsh nor ditch,
    Nor in trench anywhere,
But at the gates of Paradise
    That birk was growing fair.

'Blow up the fire, my maidens,
    Bring water from the well!
For all my house shall feast this night,
    Since my three sons are well.'

And she has made for them a bed,
    She's made it large and wide;
And she's taken her mantle her about,
    Sat down by the bedside.

Up then crew the red, red cock,
    And up and crew the grey;
The eldest to the youngest said,
    ' 'Tis time we were away.

'The cock doth crow, the day doth dawn,
    The channering worm doth chide;
If we be missed out of our place,
    A sore pain we must bide.'

channering: gnawing

'Lie still, lie still, but a little wee while,
    Lie still, if but we may;
If my mother should miss us when she wakes,
    She'll go mad ere it be day.

'Our mother has no more but us –
    See where she leans asleep,
The mantle that was about herself,
    She has wrapped it round our feet.'

O it's they have taken up their mother's mantle,
    And they've hung it on a pin:
'O long may you hang, my mother's mantle,
    Ere you wrap us again!'

'Fare you well, my mother dear,
    Farewell to barn and byre,
And fare you well, the bonny lass
    That kindles my mother's fire!'

                                        Anon.

The Two Corbies

As I was walking all alone,
I heard two corbies making their moan,
The one unto the other did say,
'Where shall we go and dine this day?'

'In behind yon old turf dyke,
I know there lies a new-slain knight,
And nobody knows that he lies there
But his hawk and his hound and his lady fair.

'His hound is to the hunting gone,
His hawk to fetch the wild-fowl home,
His lady's taken another mate,
So we may make our dinner sweet.

'You'll sit on his white neck-bone,
And I'll pick out his bonny blue e'en;
With one lock of his golden hair
We'll thatch our nest when it grows bare.

'Many a one for him makes moan,
But none shall know where he is gone;
O'er his white bones, when they are bare,
The wind shall blow for evermair.'

Anon.

corbie: carrion crow

Edward, Edward!

'Why does your brand so drip with blood,
        Edward, Edward?
Why does your brand so drip with blood,
    And why so sad go ye, O?'
'O I have killed my hawk so good,
        Mother, mother;
O I have killed my hawk so good,
    And I had no more but he, O.'

'Your hawk's blood was never so red,
        Edward, Edward;
Your hawk's blood was never so red,
    My dear son, I tell thee, O.'
'O I have killed my red-roan steed,
        Mother, mother;
O I have killed my red-roan steed,
    That went so fair and free, O.'

'Your steed was old, and ye have more,
        Edward, Edward;
Your steed was old, and ye have more,
    Some other dole ye dree, O.'
'O I have killed my father dear,
        Mother, mother;
O I have killed my father dear,
    Alas, and woe is me, O!'

brand: sword
dole ye dree: grief you suffer

'And what penance will ye do for that,
    Edward, Edward?
What penance will ye do for that,
  My dear son, now tell me, O?'
'I'll set my foot in yonder boat,
    Mother, mother,
I'll set my foot in yonder boat,
  And I'll fare o'er the sea, O.'

'And what will ye do with your towers and your hall,
    Edward, Edward?
And what will ye do with your towers and your hall,
  That were so fair to see, O?'
'I'll let them stand till down they fall,
    Mother, mother;
I'll let them stand till down they fall,
  For here never more must I be, O.'

'And what will ye leave to your bairns and your wife,
    Edward, Edward?
And what will ye leave to your bairns and your wife,
    When ye go o'er the sea, O?'
'The world's room: let them beg through life,
    Mother, mother;
The world's room: let them beg through life,
    For them never more will I see, O.'

'And what will ye leave to your own mother dear,
    Edward, Edward?
And what will ye leave to your own mother dear,
    My dear son, now tell me, O?'
'The curse of hell from me shall ye bear,
    Such counsels ye gave to me, O!'

Anon.

The Two Sisters of Binnorie

There were two sisters sat in a bower;
  Binnorie, O Binnorie;
There came a knight to be their wooer;
  By the bonny mill-dams of Binnorie.

He courted the eldest with gloves and rings,
But he loved the youngest above all things.

The eldest was vexed to despair,
And much she envied her sister fair.

The eldest said to the youngest one,
'Will ye see our father's ships come in?'

She's taken her by the lily-white hand,
And led her down to the river strand.

The youngest stood upon a stone;
The eldest came and pushed her in.

'O sister, sister, reach your hand,
And you shall be heir of half my land.

'O sister, reach me but your glove
And sweet William shall be all your love.'

'Sink on, nor hope for hand or glove!
Sweet William shall surely be my love.'

Sometimes she sank, sometimes she swam,
Until she came to the mouth of the dam.

Out then came the miller's son
And saw the fair maid swimming in.

'O father, father, draw your dam!
Here's either a mermaid or a swan.'

The miller hasted and drew his dam,
And there he found a drowned woman.

You could not see her middle small,
Her girdle was so rich withal.

You could not see her yellow hair
For the gold and pearls that clustered there.

And by there came a harper fine
Who harped to nobles when they dine.

And when he looked that lady on,
He sighed and made a heavy moan.

He's made a harp of her breast bone,
Whose sound would melt a heart of stone.

He's taken three locks of her yellow hair
And with them strung his harp so rare.

He went into her father's hall
To play his harp before them all.

But as he laid it on a stone,
The harp began to play alone.

And soon the harp sang loud and clear,
'Farewell, my father and mother dear.

'Farewell, farewell, my brother Hugh,
Farewell, my William, sweet and true.'

And then as plain as plain could be,
   (*Binnorie, O Binnorie*)
'There sits my sister who drowned me
   By the bonny mill-dams of Binnorie!'

Anon.

May Colvin

False Sir John a-wooing came,
  To a maid of beauty rare;
May Colvin was the lady's name,
  Her father's only heir.

He wooed her indoors, he wooed her out,
  He wooed her night and day;
Until he got the lady's consent
  To mount and ride away.

'Go fetch me some of your father's gold
  And some of your mother's fee,
And I'll carry you to the far Northland
  And there I'll marry thee.'

She's gone to her father's coffers,
  Where all his money lay;
And she's taken the red, and she's left the white,
  And lightly she's tripped away.

She's gone down to her father's stable,
  Where all his steeds did stand;
And she's taken the best and left the worst,
  That was in her father's land.

He rode on, and she rode on,
    They rode a long summer's day,
Until they came to a broad river,
    An arm of a lonesome sea.

'Leap off the steed,' says false Sir John
    'Your bridal bed you see
For it's seven fair maids I have drowned here,
    And the eighth one you shall be.

'Cast off, cast off your silks so fine,
    And lay them on a stone,
For they are too fine and costly
    To rot in the salt sea foam.'

'O turn about, thou false Sir John,
    And look to the leaf o' the tree;
For it never became a gentleman
    A naked woman to see.'

He's turned himself straight round about
    To look to the leaf o' the tree;
She's twined her arms about his waist,
    And thrown him into the sea.

'O hold a grip of me, May Colvin,
  For fear that I should drown;
I'll take you home to your father's gates,
  And safe I'll set you down.'

'O safe enough I am, Sir John,
  And safer I will be;
For seven fair maids have you drowned here,
  The eighth shall not be me.

'O lie you there, thou false Sir John,
  O lie you there,' said she,
'For you lie not in a colder bed
  Than the one you intended for me.'

So she went on her father's steed,
  As swift as she could away;
And she came home to her father's gates
  At the breaking of the day.

Up then spake the pretty parrot:
  'May Colvin, where have you been?
What has become of false Sir John,
  That wooed you yestere'en?'

'O hold your tongue, my pretty parrot,
　　Nor tell no tales on me;
Your cage will be made of the beaten gold
　　With spokes of ivory.'

Up then spake her father dear,
　　In the chamber where he lay:
'What ails you, pretty parrot,
　　That you prattle so long ere day?'

'There came a cat to my door, master,
　　I thought 'twould have worried me;
And I was calling on May Colvin
　　To take the cat from me.'

Anon.

Lord Lovelace

Lord Lovelace rode home from the wars,
His wounds were black as ice,
While overhead the winter sun
Hung out its pale device.

The lance was tattered in his hand,
Sundered his axe and blade,
And in a bloody coat of war
Lord Lovelace was arrayed.

And he was sick and he was sore
But never sad was he,
And whistled bright as any bird
Upon an April tree.

'Soon, soon,' he cried, 'at Lovelace Hall
Fair Ellen I shall greet,
And she with loving heart and hand
Will make my sharp wounds sweet.

'And Young Jehan the serving-man
Will bring the wine and bread,
And with a yellow link will light
Us to the bridal bed.'

But when he got to Lovelace Hall
Burned were both wall and stack,
And in the stinking moat the tower
Had tumbled on its back.

And none welcomed Lord Lovelace home
Within the castle shell,
And ravaged was the land about
That Lord Lovelace knew well.

Long in his stirrups Lovelace stood
Before his broken door,
And slowly rode he down the hill
Back to the bitter war.

Nor mercy showed he from that day,
Nor tear fell from his eye,
And rich and poor both fearful were
When Black Lovelace rode by.

This tale is true that now I tell
To woman and to man,
As Fair Ellen is my wife's name
And mine is Young Jehan.

Charles Causley

Lord Randal

'O where have you been, Lord Randal, my son?
O where have you been, my handsome young man?'
'I have been to the wild wood; mother, make my bed soon,
For I'm weary with hunting, and fain would lie down.'

'Who gave you your dinner, Lord Randal, my son?
Who gave you your dinner, my handsome young man?'
'I dined with my sweetheart; mother, make my bed soon,
For I'm weary with hunting, and fain would lie down.'

'What had you for dinner, Lord Randal, my son?
What had you for dinner, my handsome young man?
'I had eels boiled in broth; mother, make my bed soon,
For I'm weary with hunting, and fain would lie down.'

'And where are your bloodhounds, Lord Randal, my son?
And where are your bloodhounds, my handsome young man?'
'O they swelled and they died; mother, make my bed soon,
For I'm weary with hunting, and fain would lie down.'

'O I fear you are poisoned, Lord Randal, my son!
O I fear you are poisoned, my handsome young man!'
'O yes! I am poisoned; mother, make my bed soon,
For I'm sick at the heart, and I fain would lie down.'

Anon.

Barbara Allen's Cruelty

In Scarlet town, where I was born,
  There was a fair maid dwellin'
Made every youth cry 'Well-a-way!'
  Her name was Barbara Allen.

All in the merry month of May,
  When green buds they were swellin',
Young Jemmy Grove on his death-bed lay,
  For love of Barbara Allen.

He sent his man in to her then,
  To the town where she was dwellin';
'O haste and come to my master dear,
  If your name be Barbara Allen.'

So slowly, slowly rose she up,
  And slowly she came nigh him,
And when she drew the curtain by –
  'Young man, I think you're dyin'.'

'O it's I am sick and very very sick,
  And it's all for Barbara Allen.' –
'O the better for me you shall never be,
  Though your heart's blood were a-spillin'!

'O don't you mind, young man,' says she,
    'When the red wine you were fillin',
'That you made the healths go round and round,
    And slighted Barbara Allen?'

He turn'd his face unto the wall,
    And death was with him dealin':
'Adieu, adieu, my dear friends all,
    And be kind to Barbara Allen!'

As she was walking o'er the fields,
    She heard the dead-bell knellin';
And every beat the dead-bell gave
    Cried, 'Woe to Barbara Allen.'

'O mother, mother, make my bed,
    O make it soft and narrow:
My love has died for me to-day,
    I'll die for him to-morrow.

'Farewell,' she said, 'ye virgins all,
    And shun the fault I fell in:
Henceforth take warning by the fall
    Of cruel Barbara Allen.'

                                    Anon.

The Ballad of Charlotte Dymond

Charlotte Dymond, a domestic servant aged eighteen, was murdered near Rowtor Ford on Bodmin Moor on Sunday, 14th April 1844 by her young man, a crippled farm-hand, Matthew Weeks, aged twenty-two. A stone marks the spot.

It was a Sunday evening
   And in the April rain
That Charlotte went from our house
   And never came home again.

Her shawl of diamond redcloth,
   She wore a yellow gown,
She carried the green gauze handkerchief
   She bought in Bodmin town.

About her throat her necklace
   And in her purse her pay:
The four silver shillings
   She had at Lady Day.

In her purse four shillings
   And in her purse her pride
As she walked out one evening
   Her lover at her side.

Out beyond the marshes
　Where the cattle stand,
With her crippled lover
　Limping at her hand.

Charlotte walked with Matthew
　Through the Sunday mist,
Never saw the razor
　Waiting at his wrist.

Charlotte she was gentle
　But they found her in the flood
Her Sunday beads among the reeds
　Beaming with her blood.

Matthew, where is Charlotte,
　And wherefore has she flown?
For you walked out together
　And now are come alone.

Why do you not answer,
　Stand silent as a tree,
Your Sunday worsted stockings
　All muddied to the knee?

Why do you mend your breast-pleat
　With a rusty needle's thread
And fall with fears and silent tears
　Upon your single bed?

Why do you sit so sadly
　Your face the colour of clay
And with a green gauze handkerchief
　Wipe the sour sweat away?

Has she gone to Blisland
　To seek an easier place,
And is that why your eye won't dry
　And blinds your bleaching face?

'Take me home!' cried Charlotte,
　'I lie here in the pit!
A red rock rests upon my breasts
　And my naked neck is split!'

Her skin was soft as sable,
　Her eyes were wide as day,
Her hair was blacker than the bog
　That licked her life away.

Her cheeks were made of honey,
  Her throat was made of flame
Where all around the razor
  Had written its red name.

As Matthew turned at Plymouth
  About the tilting Hoe,
The cold and cunning Constable
  Up to him did go:

'I've come to take you, Matthew,
  Unto the Magistrate's door.
Come quiet now, you pretty poor boy,
  And you must know what for.'

'She is as pure,' cried Matthew,
  'As is the early dew,
Her only stain it is the pain
  That round her neck I drew!

'She is as guiltless as the day
  She sprang forth from her mother.
The only sin upon her skin
  Is that she loved another.'

They took him off to Bodmin,
    They pulled the prison bell,
They sent him smartly up to Heaven
    And dropped him down to Hell.

All through the granite kingdom
    And on its travelling airs
Ask which of these two lovers
    The most deserves your prayers.

And your steel heart search, Stranger,
    That you may pause and pray
For lovers who come not to bed
    Upon their wedding day,

But lie upon the moorland
    Where stands the sacred snow
Above the breathing river,
    And the salt sea-winds go.

                              Charles Causley

Thomas the Rhymer

True Thomas lay on Huntlie bank,
   A marvel with his eye spied he,
There he saw a lady bright
   Come riding down by the Eildon Tree.

Her skirt was of the grass-green silk,
   Her mantle of the velvet fine;
At each tuft of her horse's mane
   Hung fifty silver bells and nine.

True Thomas he pulled off his cap,
   And bowed him low down on his knee:
'Hail to thee, Mary, Queen of Heaven,
   For thy peer on earth could never be.'

'O no, O no, Thomas,' she said,
   'That name does not belong to me;
I'm but the Queen of fair Elfland,
   That am hither come to visit thee.

'Harp and carp, Thomas,' she said,
   'Harp and carp along with me;
And if you dare to kiss my lips,
   Sure of you, Thomas, I shall be.'

*Eildon Tree: the tree of magic. Here the Rhymer
uttered his prophecies
harp and carp: play and sing*

'Betide me weal, betide me woe,
    That doom shall never frighten me.'
Soon he has kissed her rosy lips,
    All underneath the Eildon Tree.

'Now you must go with me,' she said,
    'True Thomas, you must go with me:
And you must serve me seven years,
    Through weal or woe as may chance to be.'

She's mounted on her milk-white steed,
    She's taken true Thomas up behind;
And aye whenever her bridle rang,
    The steed went swifter than the wind.

O they rode on, and farther on,
    The steed went swifter than the wind,
Until they reached a desert wide,
    And living land was left behind.

'Light down, light down, now, true Thomas,
    And lean your head upon my knee;
Abide ye there a little space,
    And I will show you marvels three.

'O see ye not yon narrow road,
  So thick beset with thorns and briars?
That is the Path of Righteousness,
  Though after it but few inquires.

'And see ye not yon broad, broad road,
  That lies across the lily leven?
That is the Path of Wickedness,
  Though some do call it the Road to Heaven.

'And see ye not yon bonny road,
  That winds about the ferny brae?
That is the Road to fair Elfland,
  And you and I must go that way.

'But Thomas, you must hold your tongue,
  Whatever you may hear or see;
For speak ye word in Elfin-land,
  Ye'll never win back to your own country.'

O they rode on and farther on,
  And they waded through rivers above the knee;
And they saw neither sun nor moon,
  But they heard the roaring of the sea.

leven: ?lawn
brae: hill

At last they came to a garden green,
  And she plucked an apple that grew thereby:
'Take this for thy wages, Thomas,' she said,
  'It will give thee a tongue that can never lie.'

'My tongue is my own!' true Thomas he said,
  'A good gift you would give to me!
I could neither buy nor sell,
  At fair or mart where I might be.

'I could neither speak to prince or peer,
  Nor ask of grace from fair lady!'
'Now hold thy peace, Thomas,' she said,
  'For as I say, so must it be.'

He has gotten a coat of the smooth, smooth cloth,
  And a pair of shoes of the velvet green;
And till seven years were gone and past,
  True Thomas on earth was never seen.

Anon.

Alison Gross

O Alison Gross that lives in yon tower,
   The ugliest witch in the north country,
Has trysted me one day up to her bower,
   And many fair speeches she made to me.

She stroked my head and she combed my hair,
   And she set me down softly on her knee;
Says, 'If you will be my sweetheart so true,
   So many fine things I will give to thee.'

She showed me a mantle of red scarlet,
   With golden flowers and fringes fine;
Says, 'If you will be my sweetheart so true,
   This goodly gift it shall be thine.'

'Away, away, you ugly witch,
   Hold far away, and let me be!
I never will be your sweetheart so true,
   And I wish I were out of your company.'

She next brought a shirt of the softest silk,
   Well wrought with pearls about the band;
Says, 'If you will be my sweetheart so true,
   This goodly gift you shall command.'

trysted: invited

She showed me a cup of the good red gold,
　　Well set with jewels so fair to see;
Says, 'If you will be my sweetheart so true,
　　This goodly gift I will give to thee.'

'Away, away, you ugly witch,
　　Hold far away, and let me be!
I would not once kiss your ugly mouth
　　For all the gold in the north country.'

She's turned her right and round about,
　　And thrice she blew on a grass-green horn;
And she swore by the moon and the stars above
　　That she'd make me rue the day I was born.

Then out she has taken a silver wand,
　　And she's turned her three times round and round;
She muttered such words that my strength it failed,
　　And I fell down senseless on the ground.

She's turned me into an ugly worm,
　　And made me toddle about the tree;
And aye, on every Saturday night,
　　My sister Maisry came to me,

With silver basin and silver comb,
    To comb my head upon her knee;
But before I'd have kissed with Alison Gross,
    I'd sooner have toddled about the tree.

But as it fell out, on last Hallowe'en,
    When the Fairy Court came riding by,
The Queen lighted down on a flowery bank,
    Not far from the tree where I used to lie.

She took me up in her milk-white hand,
    And she's stroked me three times over her knee;
She changed me again to my own proper shape,
    And no more I toddle about the tree.

                                        Anon.

There was a Lady in the West

There was a lady in the west,
Lay the bank with the bonny broom.
She had three daughters of the best.
Fa lang the dillo
Fa lang the dillo, dee.

There came a stranger to the gate
And he three days and nights did wait.

The eldest daughter did ope the door,
The second set him on the floor.

The third daughter she brought a chair
And placed it that he might sit there.

'Now answer me these questions three,
Or you shall surely go with me.

'Now answer me these questions six,
Or you shall surely be Old Nick's.

'Now answer me these questions nine,
Or you shall surely be all mine.

'What is greener than the grass?
What is smoother than crystal glass?

'What is louder than a horn?
What is sharper than a thorn?

'What is brighter than the light?
What is darker than the night?

'What is keener than an axe?
What is softer than melting wax?

'What is rounder than a ring?'
'To you we thus our answers bring.

'Envy is greener than the grass,
Flattery is smoother than crystal glass.

'Rumour is louder than a horn,
Hunger is sharper than a thorn.

'Truth is brighter than the light,
Falsehood is darker than the night.

'Revenge is keener than an axe,
Love is softer than melting wax.

'The world is rounder than a ring.
To you we thus our answers bring.

'Thus you have our answers nine,
Lay the bank with the bonny broom.
And we never shall be thine.
Fa lang the dillo
Fa lang the dillo, dee.'

                                        Anon.

The False Knight upon the Road

'O where are you going?'
  Quoth the false knight upon the road.
'I'm going to the school,'
  Quoth the wee boy, and still he stood.

'What is that upon your back?'
  Quoth the false knight upon the road.
'Truly it is my books,'
  Quoth the wee boy, and still he stood.

'What's that you've got in your arm?'
  Quoth the false knight upon the road.
'Truly it's peat for the school fire,'
  Quoth the wee boy, and still he stood.

'Who owns they sheep?'
  Quoth the false knight upon the road.
'They're mine and my mother's,'
  Quoth the wee boy, and still he stood.

'How many of them are mine?'
  Quoth the false knight upon the road.
'All they that have blue tails,'
  Quoth the wee boy, and still he stood.

'I wish you were on yon tree,'
    Quoth the false knight upon the road.
'And a good ladder under me,'
    Quoth the wee boy, and still he stood.

'And the ladder for to break,'
    Quoth the false knight upon the road.
'And *you* for to fall down,'
    Quoth the wee boy, and still he stood.

'I wish you were in yon sea,'
    Quoth the false knight upon the road.
'And a good ship under me,'
    Quoth the wee boy, and still he stood.

'And the ship for to sink,'
    Quoth the false knight upon the road.
'And *you* to be drowned,'
    Quoth the wee boy, and still he stood.

'O I think I hear a bell,'
    Quoth the false knight upon the road.
'Yes, and it's ringing you to hell,'
    Quoth the wee boy, and still he stood.

                                    Anon.

King John and the Abbot of Canterbury

An ancient story I'll tell you anon,
Of a notable prince, that was called King John;
He ruled over England with main and might,
But he did great wrong, and maintained little right.

And I'll tell you a story, a story so merry,
Concerning the Abbot of Canterbury;
How for his housekeeping and high renown,
They rode post to bring him to London town.

A hundred men, as the King heard say,
The Abbot kept in his house every day;
And fifty gold chains, without any doubt,
In velvet coats waited the Abbot about.

'How now, Father Abbot? I hear it of thee,
Thou keepest a far better house than me;
And for thy housekeeping and high renown,
I fear thou work'st treason against my crown.'

'My Liege,' quoth the Abbot, 'I would it were known,
I am spending nothing but what is my own;
And I trust your grace will not put me in fear,
For spending my own true-gotten gear.'

'Yes, yes, Father Abbot, thy fault is high,
And now for the same thou needest must die.
And except thou canst answer me questions three,
Thy head struck off from thy body shall be.

'Now first,' quoth the King, 'as I sit here,
With my crown of gold on my head so fair,
Among all my liegemen of noble birth,
Thou must tell to one penny what I am worth.

'Secondly, tell me beyond all doubt,
How quickly I may ride the whole world about;
And at the third question thou must not shrink,
But tell me here truly, what do I think?'

'O, these are deep questions for my shallow wit,
And I cannot answer your Grace as yet;
But if you will give me a fortnight's space,
I'll endeavour to answer your Grace.'

'Now a fortnight's space to thee will I give,
And that is the longest thou hast to live;
For unless thou answer my questions three,
Thy life and thy lands are forfeit to me.'

Away rode the Abbot all sad at this word;
He rode to Cambridge and Oxenford;
But never a doctor there was so wise,
That could by his learning an answer devise.

Then home rode the Abbot, with comfort so cold,
And he met his shepherd, a-going to fold:
'Now good Lord Abbot, you are welcome home;
What news do you bring us from great King John?'

'Sad news, sad news, shepherd, I must give;
That I have but three days more to live.
I must answer the King his questions three.
Or my head struck off from my body shall be.

'The first is to tell him, as he sits there,
With his crown of gold on his head so fair
Among all his liegemen of noble birth,
To within one penny, what he is worth.

'The second, to tell him, beyond all doubt,
How quickly he may ride this whole world about;
And at question the third, I must not shrink,
But tell him there truly, what does he think?'

'O, cheer up, my lord; did you never hear yet
That a fool may teach a wise man wit?
Lend me your serving-men, horse, and apparel,
And I'll ride to London to answer your quarrel.

'With your pardon, it oft has been told to me
That I'm like your lordship as ever can be:
And if you will but lend me your gown,
There is none shall know us at London town.'

'Now horses and serving-men thou shalt have,
With sumptuous raiment gallant and brave;
With crozier, and mitre, and rochet, and cope,
Fit to draw near to our Father the Pope.'

'Now welcome, Sir Abbot,' the King he did say,
' 'Tis well thou'rt come back to keep thy day;
For if thou canst answer my questions three,
Thy life and thy living both saved shall be.

'And first, as thou seest me sitting here,
With my crown of gold on my head so fair,
Among my liegemen of noble birth,
Tell to one penny what I am worth.'

'For thirty pence our Saviour was sold
Among the false Jews as I have been told;
And twenty-nine is the worth of thee;
For I think thou art one penny worse than he.'

The King, he laughed, and swore by St. Bittle,
'I did not think I was worth so little!
Now secondly tell me, beyond all doubt,
How quickly I may ride this world about.'

'You must rise with the sun, and ride with the same
Until the next morning he riseth again;
And then your Grace need never doubt
But in twenty-four hours you'll ride it about.'

The King he laughed, and swore by St. John
'I did not think I could do it so soon!
Now from question the third thou must not shrink,
But tell me truly, what do I think?'

'Yea, that I shall do, and make your Grace merry:
You think I'm the Abbot of Canterbury.
But I'm his poor shepherd, as plain you may see,
That am come to beg pardon for him and for me.'

The King he laughed, and swore by the mass,
'I'll make thee Lord Abbot this day in his place!'
'Now nay, my Liege, be not in such speed;
For alas! I can neither write nor read.'

'Four nobles a week, then I'll give to thee,
For this merry jest thou hast shown to me;
And tell the old Abbot, when thou gettest home,
Thou hast brought a free pardon with thanks from King John.

Anon.

The Death of Robin Hood

When Robin Hood and Little John
  Went o'er yon bank of broom,
Said Robin Hood to Little John,
  'We have shot for many a pound.

'But I am not able to shoot one shot more,
  My proud arrows will not flee;
But I have a cousin lives down below,
  Please God, she will now bleed me.

'I will never eat nor drink,' he said,
  'Nor meat will do me good,
Till I have been to merry Kirkleys
  My veins for to let blood.

'The dame prior is my aunt's daughter,
  And nigh unto my kin;
I know she would do me no harm this day,
  For all the world to win.'

'That I advise not,' said Little John,
  'Master, by the assent of me,
Without half a hundred of your best bowmen
  You take to go with ye.'

'If thou be afeared, thou Little John,
    At home I bid thee be.'
'If you be wroth, my dear master,
    You shall never hear more of me.'

Now Robin is gone to merry Kirkleys,
    And there he knocked upon the pin;
Up then rose Dame Prioress
    And let good Robin in.

Then Robin gave to Dame Prioress
    Twenty pounds in gold,
And bade her spend while that did last,
    She should have more when she would.

'Will you please to sit down, cousin Robin,
    And drink some beer with me?'
'No, I will neither eat nor drink
    Till I am blooded by thee.'

Down then came Dame Prioress,
    Down she came full quick,
With a pair of blood-irons in her hands,
    Were wrapped all in silk.

'Set a chafing-dish to the fire,' she said,
  'And strip thou up thy sleeve.'
(I hold him but an unwise man
  That will no warning believe.)

She laid the blood-irons to Robin's vein,
  Alack, the more pity!
And pierced the vein, and let out the blood
  That full red was to see.

And first it bled the thick, thick blood,
  And afterwards the thin.
And well then knew good Robin Hood
  Treason was there within.

And there she blooded bold Robin Hood
  While one drop of blood would run;
There he did bleed the live-long day,
  Until the next at noon.

He bethought him then of the casement there,
  Being locked up in the room;
But so weak was he, he could not leap,
  He could not get him down.

He bethought him then of his bugle-horn,
    That hung low down to his knee;
He set his horn unto his mouth,
    And blew out weak blasts three.

Then Little John he heard the horn,
    Where he sat under a tree;
'I fear my master is now near dead,
    He blows so wearily.'

Little John is gone to merry Kirkleys,
    As fast as fast can be,
And when he came to merry Kirkleys
    He broke locks two or three

Until he came bold Robin unto,
    Then he fell on his knee;
'A boon, a boon!' cried Little John,
    'Master, I beg of thee!'

'What is that boon,' said Robin Hood,
    'That thou dost beg of me?'
'It is to burn fair Kirkley-hall,
    And all their nunnery.'

'Now nay, now nay,' quoth Robin Hood,
  'That boon I'll not grant thee;
I never hurt woman in all my life,
  Nor men in their company.

'I never hurt maid in all my life,
  Nor at my end shall it be,
But give me my bent bow in my hand,
  And a broad arrow I'll let flee;
And where that arrow is taken up
  There shall my grave digged be.

'Lay me a green sod under my head,
  Another at my feet,
And lay my bent bow at my side,
  Which was my music sweet;
And make my grave of gravel and green,
  Which is most right and meet.

'Let me have length and breadth enough,
  And under my head a sod;
That they may say when I am dead,
  "Here lies bold Robin Hood!" '

                                        Anon.

Sir Patrick Spens

The king sits in Dunfermline town,
   Drinking the blood-red wine;
'O where will I get a skeely skipper,
   To sail this new ship of mine?'

Then up and spake an eldern knight,
   Sat at the king's right knee;
'Sir Patrick Spens is the best sailor
   That ever sailed the sea.'

Our king has written a plain letter,
   And sealed it with his hand,
And sent it to Sir Patrick Spens,
   Was walking on the strand.

'To Noroway, to Noroway,
   To Noroway o'er the foam,
The king's daughter to Noroway,
   'Tis thou must take her home.'

The first word that Sir Patrick read
   A loud laugh laughed he,
The next word that Sir Patrick read
   The tear blinded his e'e.

skeely: skilful

'O who is this has done this deed
　And told the king of me,
To send us out this time of year
　To sail upon the sea?

'Be it wind, be it wet, be it hail, be it sleet,
　Our ship must sail the foam;
The king's daughter to Noroway,
　'Tis we must take her home.'

They hoisted their sails on a Monday morn,
　With all the speed they may;
And they have landed in Noroway,
　Upon a Wednesday.

They had not been in Noroway,
　But two weeks and a day,
When that the lords of Noroway,
　Began aloud to say,

'Ye Scottishmen spend all our king's gold,
　And all our queen's supply!'
'Ye lie, ye lie, ye liars loud,
　Full loud I hear ye lie;

'For I brought as much white money
    As keeps my men and me,
And I brought a half-bushel of good red gold
    Out o'er the sea with me.

'Make ready, make ready, my merry men all!
    Our good ship sails the morn.'
'Now ever alack, my master dear,
    I fear a deadly storm!

'I saw the new moon late yestreen
    With the old moon in her arm;
And if we go to sea, master,
    I fear we'll come to harm!'

They had not sailed a league, a league,
    A league but barely three,
When the sky grew dark, and the wind blew loud,
    And gurly grew the sea.

The anchors snapped, the topmast cracked,
    It was a deadly storm;
And the waves came over the broken ship,
    Till all her sides were torn.

gurly: rough

'O where will I get a good sailor,
  To take my helm in hand,
Till I get up to the tall topmast
  To see can I spy land?'

'O here am I, a sailor good,
  To take the helm in hand,
Till you go up to the tall topmast;
  But I fear you'll never spy land.'

He had not gone a step, a step,
  A step but barely one,
When a bolt flew out of the good ship's side,
  And the salt sea it came in.

'Go, fetch a web of the silken cloth,
  Another of the twine,
And wrap them into the good ship's side,
  And let not the sea come in.'

They fetched a web of the silken cloth,
  Another of the twine,
And they wrapped them into the good ship's side,
  But still the sea came in.

O loth, loth were our good Scots lords
   To wet their cork-heel shoon,
But long ere all the play was played
   They wet their hats aboon.

And many was the feather bed
   That floated on the foam,
And many was the good lord's son
   That never more came home.

O long, long may the ladies sit,
   With their fans into their hand,
Before they see Sir Patrick Spens
   Come sailing to the strand!

And long, long may the maidens sit,
   With their gold combs in their hair,
A-waiting for their own dear loves,
   For them they'll see no mair.

Half-o'er, half-o'er to Aberdour,
   'Tis fifty fathoms deep,
And there lies good Sir Patrick Spens
   With the Scots lords at his feet.

                    Anon.

The Inchcape Rock

No stir in the air, no stir in the sea,
The ship was as still as she could be,
Her sails from heaven received no motion,
Her keel was steady in the ocean.

Without either sign or sound of their shock
The waves flowed over the Inchcape Rock;
So little they rose, so little they fell,
They did not move the Inchcape Bell.

The Abbot of Aberbrothock
Had placed that bell on the Inchcape Rock;
On a buoy in the storm it floated and swung,
And over the waves its warning rung.

When the Rock was hid by the surge's swell
The mariners heard the warning bell;
And then they knew the perilous Rock
And blest the Abbot of Aberbrothock.

The sun in heaven was shining gay,
All things were joyful on that day;
The sea-birds screamed as they wheeled round,
And there was joyance in their sound.

The buoy of the Inchcape Bell was seen
A darker speck on the ocean green;
Sir Ralph the Rover walked his deck,
And he fixed his eye on the darker speck.

He felt the cheering power of spring;
It made him whistle, it made him sing;
His heart was mirthful to excess,
But the Rover's mirth was wickedness.

His eye was on the Inchcape float;
Quoth he, 'My men, put out the boat,
And row me to the Inchcape Rock,
And I'll plague the Abbot of Aberbrothock.'

The boat is lowered, the boatmen row,
And to the Inchcape Rock they go;
Sir Ralph bent over from the boat,
And he cut the bell from the Inchcape float.

Down sunk the bell with a gurgling sound,
The bubbles rose and burst around;
Quoth Sir Ralph, 'The next who come to the Rock
Won't bless the Abbot of Aberbrothock.'

Sir Ralph the Rover sailed away,
He scoured the seas for many a day;
And now grown rich with plundered store,
He steers his course for Scotland's shore.

So thick a haze o'erspreads the sky
They cannot see the sun on high;
The wind hath blown a gale all day,
At evening it hath died away.

On the deck the Rover takes his stand,
So dark it is he sees no land.
Quoth Sir Ralph, 'It will be lighter soon,
For there is the dawn of the rising moon.'

'Canst hear', said one, 'the breakers roar?
For methinks we should be near the shore.'
'Now where we are I cannot tell,
But I wish I could hear the Inchcape Bell.'

They hear no sound, the swell is strong;
Though the wind hath fallen they drift along,
Till the vessel strikes with a shivering shock –
'O Christ! It is the Inchcape Rock!'

Sir Ralph the Rover tore his hair;
He curst himself in his despair;
The waves rush in on every side,
The ship is sinking beneath the tide.

But even in his dying fear
One dreadful sound could the Rover hear:
A sound as if with the Inchcape Bell
The Devil below was ringing his knell.

Robert Southey

The Coasts of High Barbary

Look ahead, look astern, look the weather and the lee.
Blow high! blow low! and so sail-ed we.
I see a wreck to windward and a lofty ship to lee,
A-sailing down all on the coasts of High Barbary.

'O are you a pirate or man-o'-war?' cried we.
'O no! I'm not a pirate, but a man-o'-war,' cried he.

'Then back up your topsails and heave your vessel to,
For we have got some letters to be carried home by you.'

'We'll back up our topsails and heave our vessel to;
But only in some harbour and along the side of you.'

For broadside, for broadside, they fought all on the main,
Until at last the frigate shot the pirate's mast away.

'For quarters! for quarters!' the saucy pirate cried.
The quarters that we showed them was to sink them in the tide.

With cutlass and gun O we fought for hours three;
The ship it was their coffin, and their grave it was the sea.

But O! it was a cruel sight, and griev-ed us full sore,
Blow high! blow low! and so sail-ed we.
To see them all a-drowning as they tried to swim to shore
A-sailing down all on the coasts of High Barbary.

Anon.

The Merry Golden Tree

There was a little ship and she sailed upon the sea,
And she went by the name of 'The Merry Golden Tree',
As she sailed upon the low and the lonesome low,
As she sailed upon the lonesome sea.

There was another ship and she sailed upon the sea,
And she went by the name of 'The Turkish Robbery',
As she sailed upon the low and the lonesome low,
As she sailed upon the lonesome sea.

There was a little cabin boy upon 'The Golden Tree',
Said, 'Captain, oh Captain, what will you give to me,
If I sink them in the low and the lonesome low,
If I sink them in the lonesome sea?'

'Oh a half of my ship shall be made unto thee,
And my youngest daughter shall be wed unto thee,
If you sink them in the low and the lonesome low,
If you sink them in the lonesome sea.'

He bowed upon his breast and away swum he,
Till he come to the ship called 'The Turkish Robbery',
Gonna sink you in the low and the lonesome low,
Gonna sink you in the lonesome sea.

Then out of his pocket an instrument he drew
And he bored nine holes for to let that water through,
For to sink them in the low and the lonesome low,
For to sink them in the lonesome sea.

Oh some had hats and some had caps,
And they tried for to stop these feverish water gaps,
But he sunk them in the low and the lonesome low,
But he sunk them in the lonesome sea.

He bowed upon his breast and back swum he,
Till he come to the ship called 'The Merry Golden Tree',
As she sailed upon the low and the lonesome low,
As she sailed on the lonesome sea.

'Oh captain, oh captain, pray draw me up on board,
Oh captain, oh captain, pray give me my reward,
For I've sunk them in the low and the lonesome low,
For I've sunk them in the lonesome sea.'

'I'll never draw you up on board,
No, I've never known a cabin boy to gain such reward,
Though you sunk them in the low and the lonesome low,
Though you sunk them in the lonesome sea.'

'If it weren't for the love of your daughter and your men,
I would do unto you what I've done unto them,
I would sink you in the low and the lonesome low,
I would sink you in the lonesome sea.'

He bowed upon his breast and down sunk he,
Farewell, farewell to 'The Merry Golden Tree',
For I'm sinkin' in the low and the lonesome low,
For I'm sinkin' in the lonesome sea.

Anon.

Lord Ullin's Daughter

A chieftain to the Highlands bound
Cries 'Boatman, do not tarry!
And I'll give thee a silver pound
To row us o'er the ferry!'

'Now who be ye would cross Lochgyle,
This dark and stormy water?'
'O I'm the chief of Ulva's isle,
And this, Lord Ullin's daughter.

And fast before her father's men
Three days we've fled together,
For, should they find us in the glen,
My blood would stain the heather.

'His horsemen hard behind us ride –
Should they our steps discover,
Then who will cheer my bonny bride
When they have slain her lover?'

Out spoke the hardy Highland wight,
'I'll go, my chief, I'm ready:
It is not for your silver bright,
But for your winsome lady: –

'And, by my word! the song bird
In danger shall not tarry:
So though the waves are raging white
I'll row you o'er the ferry.'

By this the storm grew loud apace,
The water-wraith was shrieking;
And in the scowl of heaven each face
Grew dark as they were speaking.

But still, as wilder blew the wind,
And as the night grew drearer,
Adown the glen rode armed men,
Their trampling sounded nearer.

'O haste thee, haste!' the lady cries,
'Though tempests round us gather;
I'll meet the raging of the skies,
But not an angry father.'

The boat has left a stormy land,
A stormy sea before her –
When oh! too strong for human hand,
The tempest gather'd o'er her.

And still they row'd, amidst the roar
Of waters fast prevailing.
Lord Ullin reached that fatal shore –
His wrath was changed to wailing.

For, sore dismay'd, through storm and shade
His child he did discover –
One lovely hand she stretch'd for aid,
And one was round her lover.

'Come back! come back!' he cried in grief,
'Across this stormy water:
And I'll forgive your Highland chief,
My daughter! – O my daughter!'

'Twas vain: the loud waves lashed the shore,
Return or aid preventing:
The waters wild went o'er his child,
And he was left lamenting.

Thomas Campbell

I Sing of a Maiden

I sing of a maiden
  That is matchless,
King of all kings
  For her son she chose.

He came all so still
  Where his mother was,
As dew in April
  That falleth on the grass.

He came all so still
  To his mother's bower,
As dew in April
  That falleth on the flower.

He came all so still
  Where his mother lay,
As dew in April
  That falleth on the spray.

Mother and maiden
  Was never none but she;
Well may such a lady
  God's mother be.

Anon.

As Joseph was a-walking

As Joseph was a-walking
  He heard an angel sing;
'This night shall be born
  Our heavenly king;

'He neither shall be born
  In housen nor in hall,
Nor in the place of Paradise,
  But in an ox's stall.

'He neither shall be clothèd
  In purple nor in pall,
But all in fair linen,
  As wear babies all.

'He neither shall be rockèd
  In silver nor in gold,
But in a wooden cradle
  That rocks on the mould.

'He neither shall be christenèd
  In white wine or red,
But with fair spring water
  With which we were christenèd.'

Mary took her young son
   And set him on her knee;
'I pray thee now, Dear Child,
   Tell me how this world shall be.'

'O I shall be as dead, mother,
   As the stones in the wall:
O the stones in the streets, mother,
   Shall mourn for me all.

'And upon a Wednesday
   My vow I will make,
And upon Good Friday
   My death I will take.

'Upon Easter-day, mother,
   My up-rising shall be:
O the sun and the moon, mother,
   Shall both rise with me.

'The people shall rejoice,
   And the birds they shall sing,
To see the uprising
   Of the heavenly king.'

Anon.

The Bitter Withy

As it befell on a bright holiday,
Small hail from the sky did fall.
Our Saviour asked his mother dear
If he might go and play at ball.

'At ball, at ball, my own dear son,
It's time that you were gone,
But don't let me hear of any mischief
At night when you come home.'

So up the hill and down the hill
Our sweet young Saviour run,
Until he met three rich young lords.
'Good morning' to each one.

'Good morn, good morn, good morn,' said they.
'Good morning,' then said he.
'And which of you three rich young lords
Will play at ball with me?'

'Oh, we're all lords, and ladies' sons,
Born in our bower and hall,
And you are nothing but a poor maid's child,
Born in an ox's stall.'

'It's if I'm nothing but a poor maid's child
Born in an ox's stall,
I'll make you believe in your latter end
I'm an angel above you all.'

So he made him a bridge of the beams of the sun,
And over the water run he.
Them rich young lords chased after him
And drowned they were all three.

Then up the hill and down the hill
Three rich young mothers run,
Crying: 'Mary mild, fetch home your child,
For ours he's drowned each one.'

So Mary mild fetched home her child
And laid him across her knee,
And with a handful of willow twigs
She gave him slashes three.

'Ah, bitter withy, ah, bitter withy,
You've caused me to smart,
And the withy shall be the very first tree
To perish at the heart.'

Anon.

Mary, Mary Magdalene

On the south wall of the church of St. Mary Magdalene at Launceston in Cornwall is a granite figure of the saint. The children of the town say that a stone lodged on her back will bring good luck.

Mary, Mary Magdalene
Lying on the wall,
I throw a pebble on your back.
Will it lie or fall?

Send me down for Christmas
Some stockings and some hose,
And send before the winter's end
A brand-new suit of clothes.

Mary, Mary Magdalene
Under a stony tree,
I throw a pebble on your back.
What will you send me?

I'll send you for your Christening
A woollen robe to wear,
A shiny cup from which to sup,
And a name to bear.

Mary, Mary Magdalene
Lying cool as snow,
What will you be sending me
When to school I go?

I'll send a pencil and a pen
That write both clean and neat.
And I'll send to the schoolmaster
A tongue that's kind and sweet.

Mary, Mary Magdalene
Lying in the sun,
What will you be sending me
Now I'm twenty-one?

I'll send you down a locket
As silver as your skin,
And I'll send you a lover
To fit a gold key in.

Mary, Mary Magdalene
Underneath the spray,
What will you be sending me
On my wedding-day?

I'll send you down some blossom,
Some ribbons and some lace,
And for the bride a veil to hide
The blushes on her face.

Mary, Mary Magdalene
Whiter than the swan,
Tell me what you'll send me
Now my good man's dead and gone.

I'll send to you a single bed
On which you must lie,
And pillows bright where tears may light
That fall from your eye.

Mary, Mary Magdalene
Now nine months are done,
What will you be sending me
For my little son?

I'll send you for your baby
A lucky stone, and small,
To throw to Mary Magdalene
Lying on the wall.

Charles Causley

Scarborough Fair

Where are you going? To Scarborough Fair?
Parsley, sage, rosemary and thyme,
Remember me to a bonny lass there,
For once she was a true lover of mine.

Tell her to make me a cambric shirt,
Parsley, sage, rosemary and thyme,
Without any needle or thread work'd in it,
And she shall be a true lover of mine.

Tell her to wash it in yonder well,
Parsley, sage, rosemary and thyme,
Where water ne'er sprung nor a drop of rain fell,
And she shall be a true lover of mine.

Tell her to plough me an acre of land,
Parsley, sage, rosemary and thyme,
Between the sea and the salt sea strand,
And she shall be a true lover of mine.

Tell her to plough it with one ram's horn,
Parsley, sage, rosemary and thyme,
And sow it all over with one peppercorn,
And she shall be a true lover of mine.

Tell her to reap it with a sickle of leather,
Parsley, sage, rosemary and thyme,
And tie it all up with a tom tit's feather,
And she shall be a true lover of mine.

Tell her to gather it all in a sack,
Parsley, sage, rosemary and thyme,
And carry it home on a butterfly's back,
And then she shall be a true lover of mine.

Anon.

The Wraggle Taggle Gipsies

There were three gipsies a-come to my door,
And downstairs ran this a-lady, O!
One sang high, and another sang low,
And the other sang, Bonny, Bonny Biscay, O!

Then she pulled off her silk-finished gown
And put on hose of leather, O!
The ragged, ragged, rags about our door –
She's gone with the wraggle taggle gipsies, O!

It was late last night, when my lord came home,
Enquiring for his a-lady, O!
The servants said, on every hand:
'She's gone with the wraggle taggle gipsies, O!'

'O saddle to me my milk-white steed,
Go and fetch me my pony, O!
That I may ride and seek my bride,
Who is gone with the wraggle taggle gipsies, O!'

O he rode high and he rode low,
He rode through woods and copses too,
Until he came to an open field,
And there he espied his a-lady, O!

'What makes you leave your house and land?
What makes you leave your money, O?
What makes you leave your new-wedded lord;
To go with the wraggle taggle gipsies, O?'

'What care I for my house and my land?
What care I for my money, O?
What care I for my new-wedded lord?
I'm off with the wraggle taggle gipsies, O!'

'Last night you slept on a goose-feather bed,
With the sheet turned down so bravely, O!
And to-night you'll sleep in a cold open field,
Along with the wraggle taggle gipsies, O!'

'What care I for a goose-feather bed,
With the sheet turned down so bravely, O?
For tonight I shall sleep in a cold open field,
Along with the wraggle taggle gipsies, O!'

Anon.

The Cowboy's Lament

As I walked out in the streets of Laredo,
As I walked out in Laredo one day,
I spied a poor cowboy wrapped up in white linen,
Wrapped up in white linen as cold as the clay.

'Oh beat the drum slowly and play the fife lowly,
Play the Dead March as you carry me along;
Take me to the green valley, there lay the turf o'er me,
For I'm a young cowboy and I know I've done wrong.

'I see by your outfit that you are a cowboy,' –
These words he did say as I boldly stepped by –
'Come sit down beside me and hear my sad story,
I am shot in the breast and I know I must die.

'Let sixteen gamblers come handle my coffin,
Let sixteen cowboys come sing me a song.
Take me to the graveyard and lay the turf o'er me,
For I'm a poor cowboy and I know I've done wrong.

'It was once in the saddle I used to go dashing,
It was once in the saddle I used to go gay;
First to the dram-house and then to the card-house,
Got shot in the breast and I'm dying today.

'Get six jolly cowboys to carry my coffin,
Get six pretty maidens to bear up my pall.
Put bunches of roses all over my coffin,
Put roses to deaden the sods as they fall.

'Then swing your rope slowly and rattle your spurs lowly,
And give a wild whoop as you carry me along,
And in the grave throw me and roll the turf o'er me,
For I'm a young cowboy and I know I've done wrong.

'Oh bury beside me my knife and six-shooter,
My spurs on my heel, as you sing me a song,
And over my coffin put a bottle of brandy
That the cowboys may drink as they carry me along.

'Go bring me a cup, a cup of cold water
To cool my parched lips,' the cowboy then said;
Before I returned his soul had departed,
And gone to the round-up; the cowboy was dead.

We beat the drum slowly and played the fife lowly,
And bitterly wept as we bore him along;
For we all loved our comrade, so brave, young and handsome,
We all loved our comrade although he'd done wrong.

Anon.

Casey Jones

Come all you rounders, listen here,
I'll tell you the story of a brave engineer;
Casey Jones was the hogger's name,
On a six-eight-wheeler, boys, he won his fame.
Caller called Casey at half-past four,
He kissed his wife at the station door,
Mounted to the cabin with orders in his hand,
And took his farewell trip to the promised land.

Casey Jones mounted to the cabin,
Casey Jones, with his orders in his hand!
Casey Jones mounted to the cabin,
Took his farewell trip into the promised land.

'Put in your water and shovel in your coal,
Put your head out the window, watch the drivers roll,
I'll run her till she leaves the rail,
'Cause we're eight hours late with the Western Mail!'
He looked at his watch and his watch was slow,
Looked at the water and the water was low,
Turned to his fireboy and then he said,
'We're bound to reach 'Frisco, but we'll all be dead!'

Casey pulled up Reno Hill,
Tooted for the crossing with an awful shrill.
Snakes all knew by the whistle's moans
That the hogger at the throttle was Casey Jones.
He pulled up short two miles from the place,
Freight train stared him right in the face,
Turned to his fireboy, 'Sim, you'd better jump,
'Cause there's two locomotives that's going to bump!'

Casey said, just before he died,
'There's two more roads I'd like to ride.'
Fireboy asked, 'What can they be?'
'The Rio Grande and the Sante Fe.'
Mrs. Jones sat on her bed a-sighing,
Got a pink that Casey was dying,
Said, 'Hush you, children, stop your crying,
'Cause you'll get another papa on the Salt Lake line.'

>   *Casey Jones mounted to the cabin,*
>   *Casey Jones, with his orders in his hand!*
>   *Casey Jones mounted to the cabin,*
>   *Took his farewell trip into the promised land.*

Anon.

pink: telegram

The Ballad of William Sycamore (1790–1871)

My father, he was a mountaineer,
His fist was a knotty hammer;
He was quick on his feet as a running deer,
And he spoke with a Yankee stammer.

My mother, she was merry and brave,
And so she came to her labour,
With a tall green fir for her doctor grave
And a stream for her comforting neighbour.

And some are wrapped in the linen fine,
And some like a godling's scion;
But I was cradled on twigs of pine
In the skin of a mountain lion.

And some remember a white starched lap
And a ewer with silver handles;
But I remember a coonskin cap
And the smell of bayberry candles.

The cabin logs, with the bark still rough,
And my mother who laughed at trifles,
And the tall, lank visitors, brown as snuff,
With their long, straight squirrel rifles.

I can hear them dance, like a foggy song,
Through the deepest one of my slumbers,
The fiddle squeaking the boots along
And my father calling the numbers.

The quick feet shaking the puncheon-floor,
The fiddle squeaking and squealing,
Till the dried herbs rattled above the door
And the dust went up to the ceiling.

There are children lucky from dawn till dusk,
But never a child so lucky!
For I cut my teeth on 'Money Musk'
In the Bloody Ground of Kentucky!

When I grew as tall as the Indian corn,
My father had little to lend me,
But he gave me his great, old powder-horn
And his woodsman's skill to befriend me.

With a leather shirt to cover my back,
And a redskin nose to unravel
Each forest sign, I carried my pack
As far as a scout could travel.

Till I lost my boyhood and found my wife,
A girl like a Salem clipper!
A woman straight as a hunting-knife
With eyes as bright as the Dipper!

We cleared our camp where the buffalo feed,
Unheard-of streams were our flagons;
And I sowed my sons like apple-seed
On the trail of the Western wagons.

They were right, tight boys, never sulky or slow,
A fruitful, a goodly muster.
The eldest died at the Alamo
The youngest fell with Custer.

The letter that told it burned my hand,
Yet we smiled and said, 'So be it!'
But I could not live when they fenced the land,
For it broke my heart to see it.

I saddled a red, unbroken colt
And rode him into the day there;
And he threw me down like a thunderbolt
And rolled on me as I lay there.

The hunter's whistle hummed in my ear
As the city-men tried to move me,
And I died in my boots like a pioneer
With the whole wide sky above me.

Now I lie in the heart of the fat, black soil,
Like the seed of a prairie-thistle;
It has washed my bones with honey and oil
And picked them clean as a whistle.

And my youth returns, like the rains of spring,
And my sons like the wild geese flying;
And I lie and hear the meadow-lark sing
And have much content in my dying.

Go play with the towns you have built of blocks,
The towns where you would have bound me!
I sleep in my earth like a tired fox,
And my buffalo have found me.

Stephen Vincent Benét

Ballad

Oh come, my joy, my soldier boy,
With your golden buttons, your scarlet coat,
Oh let me play with your twinkling sword
And sail away in your wonderful boat!

The soldier came and took the boy.
Together they marched the dusty roads.
Instead of war, they sang at Fairs,
And mended old chairs with river reeds.

The boy put on a little black patch
And learned to sing on a tearful note;
The soldier sold his twinkling sword
To buy a crutch and a jet-black flute.

And when the summer sun rode high
They laughed the length of the shining day;
But when the robin stood in the hedge
The little lad's courage drained away.

Oh soldier, my soldier, take me home
To the nut-brown cottage under the hill.
My mother is waiting, I'm certain sure;
She's far too old to draw at the well!

As snowflakes fell the boy spoke so,
For twenty years, ah twenty years;
But a look in the soldier's eyes said no,
And the roads of England were wet with tears.

One morning, waking on the moors,
The lad laughed loud at the corpse by his side.
He buried the soldier under a stone,
But kept the flute to soothe his pride.

The days dragged on and he came to a town,
Where he got a red jacket for chopping wood;
And meeting a madman by the way,
He bartered the flute for a twinkling sword.

And so he walked the width of the land
With a warlike air and a jaunty word.
Looking out for a likely lad,
With the head of a fool and the heart of a bard.

Henry Treece

O what is that sound?

O what is that sound which so thrills the ear
   Down in the valley drumming, drumming?
Only the scarlet soldiers, dear,
   The soldiers coming.

O what is that light I see flashing so clear
   Over the distance brightly, brightly?
Only the sun on their weapons, dear,
   As they step lightly.

O what are they doing with all that gear,
   What are they doing this morning, this morning?
Only their usual manoeuvres, dear,
   Or perhaps a warning.

O why have they left the road down there
   Why are they suddenly wheeling, wheeling?
Perhaps a change in their orders, dear.
   Why are you kneeling?

O haven't they stopped for the doctor's care,
   Haven't they reined their horse, their horses?
Why, they are none of them wounded, dear,
   None of these forces.

O is it the parson they want, with white hair,
  Is it the parson, is it, is it?
No, they are passing his gateway, dear,
  Without a visit.

O it must be the farmer who lives so near.
  It must be the farmer so cunning, so cunning?
They have passed the farmyard already, dear,
  And now they are running.

O where are you going? Stay with me here!
  Were the vows you swore deceiving, deceiving?
No, I promised to love you, dear,
  But I must be leaving.

O it's broken the lock and splintered the door,
  O it's the gate where they're turning, turning:
Their boots are heavy on the floor
  And their eyes are burning.

                                        W. H. Auden

Index of First Lines

Acknowledgements

For permission to use copyright material the editor and publishers are indebted to the following:

David Higham Associates Ltd. for the following poems by Charles Causley: 'Lord Lovelace' and 'Mary, Mary Magdalene' from *Figgie Hobbin* (Macmillan & Co. Ltd.) and 'The Ballad of Charlotte Dymond' from *Johnny Allelulia* (Rupert Hart-Davies Ltd.); Faber & Faber Ltd. for 'Ballad' by Henry Treece from *The Black Seasons* and 'O what is that sound?' by W. H. Auden from *Collected Shorter Poems 1927–57*; Holt, Rinehart and Winston for 'The Ballad of William Sycamore' from *Poems and Ballads*.

Every effort has been made to trace the owners of copyright and we apologise to any copyright holder whose rights we may unwittingly have infringed.